KINGDOMS AND EMPIRES

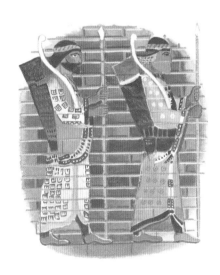

KINGDOMS AND EMPIRES

PETER
BEDRICK
BOOKS

This edition published in 2002 by Peter Bedrick Books
an imprint of McGraw-Hill Children's Publishing
8787 Orion Place
Columbus, OH 43240

Copyright © 2001 Octopus Publishing Group Ltd.

The material in this book has previously appeared in
History of the World (Bounty, Octopus Publishing Group Ltd, 2001)

ISBN 1-57768-951-8

Printed in China

McGraw-Hill
Children's Publishing
A Division of The McGraw-Hill Companies

PHOTOGRAPHIC CREDITS

8 (B/R) Diego Lezanna/CORBIS; 18 (B/R) Adam Woolfitt/CORBIS; 47 (C/L) Werner Forman/CORBIS. All
other images from the Miles Kelly Archive.

QUOTATION ACKNOWLEDGMENTS

Pages 23 (translated by Dell R. Hales), 27 (translated by Frank O'Connor),
41 (translated by Dennis Tedlock), published in *World Poetry* by W. W. Norton and Company; page 29 *The Aeneid*,
translated by W.F. Jackson Knight, published by Penguin; page 11, *The Histories*, translated by Aubrey De
Sélincourt, published by Penguin; page 15, *The History of the Peleponnesian War*, translated by Rex Warner, published
by Penguin; page 39 published in the *Oxford Dictionary of Quotations* by the Oxford University Press; page 45,
extract from *Murasaki Shikibu, her Diary and Poetic Memoirs*, translated by Richard Bowring, published by Princeton
University Press.

Every effort has been made to trace all copyright holders and obtain permissions. The editor and publishers sin-
cerely apologize for any inadvertent errors or omissions and will be happy to correct them in any future editions.

Contents

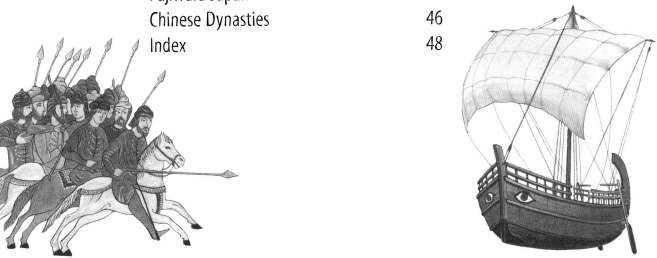

By about 1000 BC, the civilizations of North Africa and the Near East had begun to exchange ideas. These civilizations were linked by trade routes. New ideas traveled between civilizations as groups of people moved around the world, for trade and also for conquest.

Empires East and West

People moved overland with their animal herds or set sail in ships to settle in new lands. In Egypt, China, India, and Mesopotamia civilization had introduced new ways of life. These involved farming, living in towns, trade, organized religion, and government by kings. The people who shared these common experiences were more likely to adapt to life under a common ruler, and this encouraged the growth of new empires.

Building empires

These empires brought together different peoples who spoke different languages and sometimes lived far apart. Strong rulers, backed by powerful armies, struggled to win empires and then hold them together. Sometimes the unifying force in building an empire was the will of a dynamic ruler, such

as Alexander the Great. At other times it was the power of armies, religious zeal, or the attraction of a way of life that offered greater peace and prosperity for all.

America, Australasia, and Africa south of the Sahara were still untouched by the civilizations of Europe and Asia. However, as contacts between the empires of the East and the West grew, the chain of civilization added new links. By about AD 100, when the Roman Empire was at its height, civilization in one form or another existed from western Europe across to China in the East.

Cultural areas

The empires of Greece, Asoka's India, Han China, and Rome created "cultural areas" that were larger than any earlier in history. Inside these empires ideas, knowledge, religious beliefs, and culture could spread and take root. Their effect on the history of the world has been to leave behind a cultural legacy that is still very much part of our lives today.

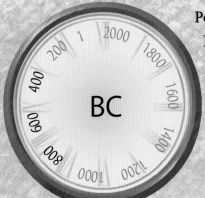

BC

Persia grew from the rubble of the defeated Assyrian Empire. In 612 BC Nineveh, the Assyrian capital, fell. This left Babylon and Media to wrestle over the remains of the empire.

The Persian Empire

In 550 BC the Persian king Cyrus defeated the Medes and made himself ruler of a new empire. It was known as the Achaemenid Empire, after an ancestor of Cyrus who was named Achaemenes.

The Persians
The Persians were Iranians, whose ancestors had ridden on horses from the plains of central Asia. Many Persians lived as nomads, but their rulers built mighty cities with stone palaces. The greatest Persian city was Persepolis, built to the orders of the king, Darius I, in about 518 BC. A Persian man could have several wives, but the king could marry only women selected from six noble families.

The god of light
The Persians believed in sun and sky gods, and gods of nature. They built no temples, but worshipped on the tops of mountains. The chief

Medes set up a kingdom in what is now Iran.	700 BC
Cyrus the Great rebels against the Medes. Achaemenid Empire founded.	550 BC
Cyrus conquers Lydia.	545 BC
Cambyses, son of Cyrus, defeats the Egyptian king Psamtik III.	525 BC
Darius I becomes ruler of Persia.	522 BC
Battle of Marathon halts Persian invasion of Greece.	490 BC
Battles of Thermopylae and Salamis. Greeks defeat Xerxes, son of Darius I.	480 BC
Alexander the Great conquers Persia.	331 BC

△ The ruins of Persepolis, the capital of the Persian Empire, lie near the modern city of Shiraz, in southwest Iran. Part of the ruined palace of Darius I is still standing.

△ Ten thousand soldiers called the Immortals formed the core of the Persian army. Each spearman or archer was instantly replaced if killed or sick.

Mithra

Although Ahura Mazda was the chief god of Persia, many people also worshipped Mithra, seen here killing a bull as a sacrifice to renew life. Later, Mithraism was popular among the Romans.

god of Persia was Ahura Mazda, a winged god of light. Many people followed the teachings of the prophet Zarathustra (Zoroaster), who lived between 1400 and 1000 BC. He taught that life was a struggle between good (light) and evil (darkness).

△ Darius I ruled Persia from 521 to 486 BC. He encouraged trade through the use of coins and new canals.

War and empire

The Persians were good fighters, with cavalry and iron weapons, and their military energy proved too strong for their neighbors. The great soldier Cyrus conquered Lydia and the Greek colonies in Asia Minor, and won control of Babylon, too. When he died, his son Cambyses conquered Egypt. Civil war broke out after Cambyses' death, but order was restored by Darius, a relative of Cambyses.

The wars with Greece

Darius was an able administrator. He organized the empire into provinces, each governed by a satrap. A satrap was like a king, but the king of kings was the emperor himself, whose word was final. Darius and his son Xerxes tried to bring Greece within the empire, but failed. The Greeks beat the Persians at the battle of Marathon in 490 BC, and the naval defeat at Salamis was a major setback. But Persia stayed rich and powerful until 331 BC, when it was conquered by Alexander the Great.

◁ The Persian Empire stretched from North Africa as far as the Caucasus Mountains in the north, and the borders of India in the east.

BC

2000 1800 1600 1400 1200 1000 800 600 400 200

Ancient Greece, practically cut off by sea from Asia Minor (Turkey), had escaped conquest by the warlike empires of the Near East. In this land of mountains and plains, small city-states grew up independent and proud.

The Rise of Greece

Farmland was so scarce that many Greeks left home and wandered in search of new lands. They built fine oared ships, and Greek colonists and traders could be found from one end of the Mediterranean Sea to the other.

Greek cities

Living in their small cities, the Greeks developed a remarkable system of government. Each city was enclosed by a wall for protection. Inside the city was a fort, called an *acropolis*, on a hill or mountain top. An open space, the *agora*, was used as a market and meeting place, where the men of the city met to agree how the city should be governed.

Athens and Sparta

The two states of Athens and Sparta became rivals. Athens was rich and cultured. Its citizens included astronomers, mathematicians, thinkers, writers, and artists. This was a society with slaves, but its finest rulers, such as Pericles (from about 495 to 429 BC) had vision, and its government was the first real democracy – although only men could take part.

Mycenean culture draws to a close in Greece.	1200 BC
First recorded Olympic Games.	776 BC
Nobles overthrow kings in city-states.	750 BC
Greeks found colonies around the Mediterranean Sea.	500s BC
Athens becomes a democracy, with a council of 500 men to govern it.	508 BC
Greeks defeat Persian invasions.	490–479 BC
Start of Athens' Golden Age under Pericles.	477 BC
War between Sparta and Athens, won by Sparta.	431–404 BC

▷ In 480 BC the Greek fleet defeated the Persians at the battle of Salamis. Arrows, stones, and spears rained between the ships, but the Greeks' key weapon was the ramming power of their galleys, driven at speed by banks of rowers.

△ Greek foot soldiers were called hoplites. A man had to buy his own armor, made of bronze. On the march, a slave would carry the heavy armor for his master.

Phalanx

In battle, hoplites (foot soldiers) marched in a tight group called a phalanx. Each rank kept in formation, with shields before them and their long spears pointed at the enemy as they advanced.

Athens had the best navy in Greece. Sparta had the best army. Sparta's economy, like that of Athens, was based on slave workers. There was no democracy. Sports were encouraged, and girls as well as boys were expected to be fit and athletic. Sparta was like an army camp, in which everyone was expected to obey. Boys as young as seven were taken from home and trained to be soldiers.

War with Persia

Only fear of foreign invasion made Athens and Sparta fight side by side, as they did to drive off the Persians. First Darius of Persia, and then his son Xerxes, tried to conquer Greece.

The Greeks fought desperately, at Marathon and at Thermopylae, where a small Spartan rearguard held off the Persian army. The naval victory at Salamis and the land battle of Plataea saved Greece from becoming part of the Persian Empire.

Under Pericles, Athens enjoyed a "Golden Age". The city was rebuilt, and the Parthenon temple was erected on the Acropolis. But still Athens and Sparta could not live together in peace. A war between them, called the Peloponnesian War, lasted 27 years. Athens was brought to its knees and was never the same again.

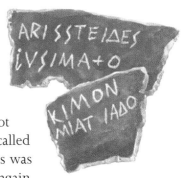

△ Broken pieces of pottery were used for letter-writing in the Greek world. Clay fragments are still found today, with business notes written on them.

Herodotus... here displays his inquiry so that great and marvelous deeds – some displayed by Greeks, some by barbarians – may not be without their glory.

THE HISTORIES, HERODOTUS (c. 485-45 BC)

Herodotus aimed to record the causes of these wars, as well as the wars themselves.

BC

In many ways, ancient Greece was the birthplace of Western civilization. In the small Greek cities, and especially in Athens, people gathered to discuss new ideas. The word "philosophy" comes from two Greek words meaning love of wisdom, and it is to the Greeks that we owe many of our ideas about beauty, justice, and government.

Greek Art and Science

First record of Olympic Games.	776 BC
Iliad and Odyssey stories first collected.	700 BC
Start of Athens' Golden Age.	477 BC
The Parthenon in Athens is completed.	432 BC
Birth of the philosopher Plato.	429 BC
Writings of Herodotus, called the "Father of History."	400s BC
Death of Socrates.	399 BC
Birth of philosopher and scientist Aristotle.	384 BC

The Greeks were never united as one nation, but they shared the same language and religion, and many similar ideas about the world.

Science and philosophy

The ancient Greeks were pioneers in medicine, mathematics, and science. They looked at the world in the light of logic and reason and made some fundamental discoveries. In the 400s BC Democritus declared

△ In a Greek theater the actors performed on a flat platform called the orchestra. Audiences sat in the open air, on a hillside, although there were seats, and some people brought their own cushions. Audiences might watch four plays in a single day.

that everything was made of atoms. Aristarchus of Samos (200s BC) knew the Earth was round, and even suggested that it traveled around the Sun.

The names of great Greek scientists such as Archimedes are familiar to this day. Socrates, Plato, and Aristotle were three of the greatest philosophers of that, or any other, age. But the common people were often suspicious of their questioning and free thinking. Socrates was sentenced to death in 399 BC for his views.

The gods

The Greeks believed in many gods. Each city had its own protector god or goddess, and families made offerings to household gods too. The gods were thought to live on Mount Olympus, under the rule of Zeus, the king of the gods. Greek gods were immortal, but they had human characteristics too – such as displaying love and jealousy.

Art and literature

The Greeks built many beautiful temples to their gods. They developed an elegant architecture based on mathematical rules and the use of three styles for the stone columns that are a feature of many Greek buildings.

Greek sculptors portrayed the human body in superb lifelike detail. Music also flourished, often accompanying dances or stories. The most famous stories were the heroic tales of Homer, but the Greeks also invented theater as we know it, and some of their plays are still performed, in many languages other than Greek.

△ *The Parthenon in Athens was built to honor the city's protector, the goddess Athene. Her gold and ivory decorated statue was inside the great hall, enclosed by columns which supported the roof like a forest of stone trees.*

△ *Greek actors wore masks to show what kind of character (comic or tragic) they played. The finest play-writers were the Athenian dramatists Aeschylus, Sophocles, Euripides (who wrote tragedies), and Aristophanes (who wrote comedies).*

Olympic Games

The Olympic Games were first recorded in 776 BC. People from all over Greece came to take part in or watch the Games, held every four years at Olympia. Sports such as running and discus throwing were to honor Zeus. The winners received crowns of olive leaves.

BC

The Greek way of life spread around the Mediterranean, as traders and colonists settled in new places. The Greeks were scornful of foreigners, calling them "barbarians". Yet Greek culture could be found across southern Europe and North Africa, far away from Greece itself.

Daily Life and Trade in Greece

Greeks begin to settle in colonies outside Greece.	750 BC
Colonists found city-states in Sicily, Crete, Cyprus, and along the coast of Africa.	750–600 BC
Greek colonists establish the city of Massilia (modern Marseilles).	c. 600 BC
Greeks begin to use coins minted from silver.	500 BC
Classical period of Greek civilization.	500–336 BC
The Peloponnesian War between Athens and Sparta.	431–404 BC
Macedonians defeat the Greeks.	338 BC

Greek homes were built around a central courtyard, cool and airy, where the family slaves prepared food on an open fire and there was a small shrine to the household god. Many houses were made without windows in the outer walls. This design kept out both the hot sun and thieves.

△ In a Greek country house, the family relaxed in a shady courtyard during the heat of the day. People ate with their fingers, lying on wooden couches, as slaves brought in the dishes and a musician played on pipes or the lyre. Men and women wore a chiton, a cloth square draped over the body and fastened by a pin at the shoulder.

Business in the town

Greek towns were a center for government, religion, and trade. In the town's marketplace, farmers sold produce such as cheese, wheat, meat, eggs, sheepskins, and olive oil. Fast-food sellers did a brisk lunchtime trade in sausages and pancakes. In the dusty lanes around the

△ Much of what we know about how the Greeks lived comes from pictures on vases. The pictures show wars and stories from mythology, but also daily activities such as hunting, farming, and fishing.

Cargo ships

Greek ships were wooden, with one square sail. Cargo ships were rounder and slower than war galleys, and often had no oars. In ships with no deck, skins or cloths covered the cargo.

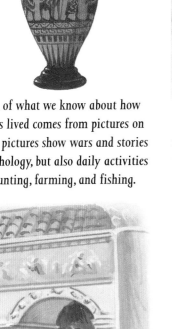

marketplace, skilled craftworkers carried on their businesses. They included sandal-makers, potters, tanners (who prepared animal skins), armorers, blacksmiths, and jewelers.

Farming and fishing

Wherever they settled, Greek farmers relied on three main crops: grapes, olives, and grain. Oxen pulled wooden plows, but much of the work of sowing and harvesting was done by hand. Grapes were made into wine. Wine and olive oil were stored in large two-handled jars called amphoras. Olive oil was used for cooking, as a fuel in lamps, and for washing (the Greeks did not use soap).

Most colonies were near the sea, and fishermen sold freshly caught fish in the market. Greek colonists enjoyed stories about sea creatures, sea gods, and the heroic legends of "the old country" – the peninsula of mainland Greece.

Traders

Greek traders sailed into the Black Sea and along the coast of North Africa. Merchant ships probably went beyond the Mediterranean, as far north as Britain. Trade with the "barbarians" (people who spoke no Greek) was done by silent exchange of goods, more being offered until both parties were happy with the deal.

Thucydides the Athenian wrote the history of the war fought between Athens and Sparta in the belief that it was going to be a great war.

HISTORY OF THE PELOPONNESIAN WAR, THUCYDIDES

The Greek historian Thucydides fought in the Peloponnesian War before writing his history.

△ A portrait of a Greek woman on a fragment of pottery. Greek women spent most of their time around the home, organizing the household and supervising the family's slaves.

One man took the Greek world into a new age, looking east towards Asia. He was Alexander of Macedonia, known to history as Alexander the Great.

Alexander the Great

Alexander was the son of the soldier-king Philip of Macedonia and Olympias, princess of Epirus. Philip's power had grown while Athens and Sparta were at war. He made his small northern kingdom a power to be feared. The Macedonian army joined with the Greeks in 338 BC to defeat the Persians.

The victory against the Persians brought unity, but in Philip's moment of triumph he was cut down by an assassin. His son Alexander, only 20, became king. Alexander had been taught by the wise scholar Aristotle and had shown a love for learning. But his greatest gift was ruthless generalship. His first act was to crush a revolt by the people of Thebes to secure his grip on Greece.

Alexander's campaigns

In just 13 years, Alexander led his army out of Europe and into Asia. He started off with 35,000 men. First, he crushed the might of Persia and swept through Syria into Egypt. There he was welcomed as a liberator from Persian rule. He founded the city of Alexandria, which became one of the great cities of learning and trade of the ancient world.

From Egypt, Alexander marched into Mesopotamia and Babylonia. The Persians had regrouped, but he defeated their army at Gaugamela. Alexander burned the Persian city of Persepolis, and shortly

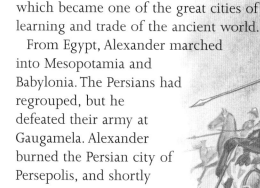

Philip II becomes king of Macedonia.	359 BC
Birth of Alexander.	356 BC
Philip defeats Persians at battle of Chaeronea.	338 BC
Philip is murdered. Alexander becomes king of Macedonia.	336 BC
Battle of Issus. Alexander defeats the Persians.	333 BC
Alexander conquers Persian Empire.	331 BC
Alexander's army enters India.	326 BC
Death of Alexander.	323 BC
Separate states emerge across the empire.	311 BC

▷ On his horse Bucephalus, Alexander leads his troops into battle at Issus in 333 BC. The horse was said to be too spirited and wild until tamed by Alexander.

△ *Alexander, shown here, believed that the Greek hero Achilles was his ancestor. He learned by heart the account of Achilles' deeds in the epic poem, the Iliad.*

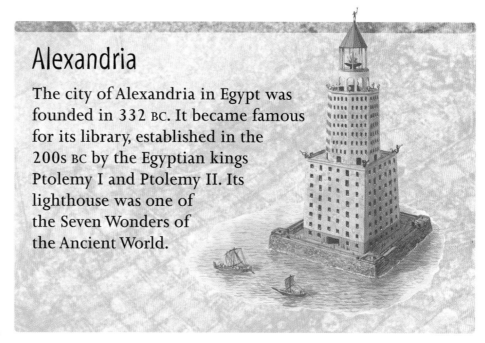

Alexandria

The city of Alexandria in Egypt was founded in 332 BC. It became famous for its library, established in the 200s BC by the Egyptian kings Ptolemy I and Ptolemy II. Its lighthouse was one of the Seven Wonders of the Ancient World.

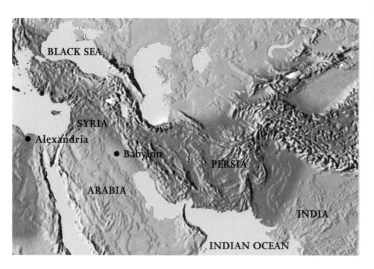

△ *Alexander imposed a single system of money throughout his lands. He was keen to promote trade and commerce across the empire too.*

afterwards the Persian king Darius was killed by his own side.

Afghanistan and India

This astonishing campaign took Alexander's army eastward into Afghanistan and as far north as Tashkent in central Asia, before he turned south toward India. In 326 BC Alexander entered what is now Pakistan and defeated the Indian king Porus. He hoped to find the mythical river Ocean, which encircled the world, but his troops would go no farther. They endured a terrible return journey across the desert of Gedrosia.

The world empire

Alexander decided to make Babylon the capital of his new "world empire." He married a Persian princess and hired soldiers of all nationalities. Everywhere he went, Greek ideas went too. Alexander was planning new conquests when he became ill and died in Babylon, just before his 33rd birthday.

Without Alexander's genius, his empire soon broke up into smaller states ruled by his generals. The strongest of these were Macedonia, Egypt, and the Asian kingdom of Seleucus Nicator.

◁ *Alexander's empire stretched from Greece to North Africa and as far east as India and Afghanistan. He ruled most of what was then thought of as "the civilized world." After his death, Alexander was buried in the city of Alexandria.*

BC

By about 600 BC India was a jigsaw puzzle of kingdoms and tribal states. In the state of Kapilavastu, Gautama Buddha, founder of one of the world's great religions, was born in about 566 BC.

New Empires in India

Most people in India at that time followed the ancient religious beliefs of Hinduism. However, the teachings of Buddha found favor with powerful rulers, and Buddhism spread quickly in India.

The rise of Chandragupta

By the 400s BC the most powerful state in India was the kingdom of Magadh which had its capital at Patna. Yet its control was weakening.
It is said that while Alexander the Great was marching into India in 325 BC, he met a young Indian ruler named Chandragupta Maurya. Chandragupta also had ambition. He seized the throne of Magadha and took

Birth of Buddha.	566 BC
Chandragupta rules small kingdom of Nanda.	321 BC
Alexander the Great invades India.	326 BC
Chandragupta wins control of Greek-held lands in India and Afghanistan.	303 BC
Bindusara succeeds his father Chandragupta.	297 BC
Asoka Maurya becomes emperor.	272 BC
Asoka conquers Kalinga (Orissa) and becomes a Buddhist.	261 BC
Death of Asoka.	232 BC

△ A detail of stone carving on the Buddhist stupa at Sanchi in India, dating from the 100s BC. It shows a parade with musicians and a ruler being driven in a two-horse chariot.

△ Buddhism is still one of the world's foremost religions, with devotees all over the modern world.

△ The extent of the Mauryan Empire during the reign of Asoka. He extended the limits of the empire until most of India was under Mauryan rule.

△ The carved stone lions on the pillar at Sarnath have become a national emblem for India.

Asoka

Asoka was probably the greatest ruler of ancient India. He became a vegetarian after adopting Buddhism and tried to follow Buddha's teachings of non-violence. After years of soldiering and killing, Asoka believed that everyone should respect all living things. He travelled in his empire, hearing the ideas and problems of his subjects.

advantage of the upheaval caused by Alexander's campaigns to seize a large chunk of territory in the north.

The Mauryan Empire

So began the Mauryan Empire. Chandragupta's son Bindusara continued and extended his conquests. The old capital of Patna (then called Pataliputra) was now the center of an empire that stretched from the Arabian Sea in the west to the Bay of Bengal in the east. Only the southern tip of the Indian subcontinent lay outside its territory.

Emperor Asoka

Chandragupta's grandson Asoka was the greatest emperor of ancient India. He took government very seriously, reforming taxes, encouraging trade and farming, and building walled cities with pleasant houses and paved streets. His officials traveled the country, building roads (including what Indians now know as the Great Trunk Road) and collecting taxes from peasant farmers in villages.

Asoka was born a Hindu, but he became a Buddhist. He then gave up war, sickened by the slaughter he had seen during his conquest of Orissa in the southeast. He urged his people to be tolerant of others and to respect all life.

Asoka's laws

Asoka made new laws and had them inscribed on stone pillars set up all across his empire. There are ten still standing today, the most famous at Sarnath near the Hindu holy city of Benares (Varanasi). The tall pillar at Sarnath is topped with four carved lions and four wheels. The wheel, often referred to as the "wheel of life," is an important symbol of Buddhism.

Peoples all over the world formed systems of beliefs in powers greater than their own. The earliest religions were connected with the forces of nature – the sun, the moon, wind, water, rocks and trees – and with animals.

Eastern Religions

The great religions of the world all began in Asia. Three of them – Judaism, Christianity, and Islam – began in the same area of west Asia. Hinduism and Buddhism began in India.

In the civilizations of the ancient world, the king was often seen as the gods' representative. The god-king defended his people. The Egyptians believed in many gods, and in a life after death. One pharaoh, Akhenaton, tried to replace the old gods with a 'one-god' faith based on sun worship. The experiment was short-lived.

Rig Vedas, earliest Hindu holy songs, written in India.	1500 BC
Jews leave Egypt (the Exodus). Moses receives the Ten Commandments.	1200 BC
Hindu Upanishads, or holy books, name a supreme spirit called Brahman.	700 BC
Zarathrustra (Zoroaster) in Persia.	c. 600s BC
The scholar Confucius teaches in China.	500s BC
Lao-tzu writes the Tao Te Ching, about the unity of all things in nature.	500s BC
Jainism, in India, founded by a wise man named Mahavira.	500 BC
Buddhism spreads in India after Asoka becomes a Buddhist.	200s BC

△ Buddhism was taught by a prince named Gautama Buddha. In this picture he is shown meditating under a shady bodhi tree in an Indian village.

20

△ Hindu pilgrims came to bathe in the waters of the holy river Ganges, as people still do today.

△ Hindu sculptures of gods and goddesses are full of energy. The four-armed Vishnu is the preserver of the Universe. He is one of Hinduism's two main gods – the other is Shiva.

India

Hinduism is the oldest of the Asian beliefs. There are many Hindu gods, and many rules that govern foods, behavior, festivals, and even which jobs people may do.

Buddhism began in India in the 500s BC and was later spread by missionaries to Burma and China. In its birthplace of India, Buddhism practically died out. It was different from other religions in having no god or gods. Its followers were taught to escape the sufferings of life by desiring nothing. Another Indian religion, Jainism, forbade its followers to kill any living thing, even an insect.

Judaism

The Jews were the first people in Europe and Asia to put their faith in one god. They believed that they were a chosen people, who owed their escape from slavery in Egypt and Babylon to a supreme God whom they called Yahweh (the Lord). God gave the Ten Commandments (laws) to Moses, and prophets delivered messages from God. Jews believed that God would send a messiah, or saviour, to bring justice and peace. Later, followers of Jesus Christ, a Jew, believed he was the Messiah (the Son of God).

Confucius

In China, people worshipped their ancestors and nature spirits. In the 500s BC, a scholar named Confucius taught a system of "right behavior" which has influenced Chinese government and society ever since. He taught loyalty to the family, worship of ancestors, and obedience to the laws of society.

△ A bronze statue of Buddha. The name Buddha means "the enlightened one."

The first emperor of China, Shih Huang-di, created enormous upheaval. The building of the Great Wall was just one sign of this upheaval, for the emperor was a ruthless tyrant. Millions of poor Chinese were forced to work as laborers on the Great Wall and other vast building projects.

Han Rule in China

End of the Qin dynasty.	206 BC
Liu Pang becomes the first Han emperor.	202 BC
Start of Wu-ti's reign. Wars against the Hun.	140 BC
Wang Mang becomes emperor, briefly founding the Hsin dynasty.	AD 9
Huns raid China and burn Chang-an.	AD 23
Han dynasty restored by emperor Liu Hsiu.	AD 25
Buddhism has reached China by this time.	AD 100
Han power begins to decline.	AD 125
End of the Han dynasty.	AD 220

Only four years after the emperor's death, the army and the mass of peasants were up in arms. From this rebellion emerged a new dynasty, the Han. The first Han emperor was Liu Pang, a minor official turned soldier, whose parents had been peasants themselves.

The Han emperors

The Han rulers made the city of Chang-an their capital. It was defended by thick walls, 60 feet high in places. The emperor lived in a magnificent palace, among his wives, concubines, courtiers, and guards.

Chinese rulers were superstitious, employing court magicians and fortune-tellers. During the period of Han rule, large stone statues were placed outside tombs. There were also enormous figures of Buddha, for Buddhism reached China in the first century AD.

Most ordinary people lived in one-room shacks and were very poor. Merchants were not allowed to live within the city walls. They were considered inferior to wheat farmers or women who reared silkworms.

China's trade links

It was during the Han dynasty that Chinese traders first had regular

△ A bustling street in the Chinese city of Chang-an (modern Xian). Traders regulated by city officials sold everything from livestock to jewelery. Scribes, artists, and craftworkers were kept busy in what was, in the 100s BC, probably the world's biggest city.

△ These soldiers are part of the huge army of terracotta figures buried near the tomb of the first Chinese emperor, Shi Huang-di. As well as thousands of warriors, the burial army also included clay horses and chariots. The figures were placed in three pits inside the large complex surrounding the emperor's tomb.

The Silk Road

The Silk Road stretched 2,500 miles across central Asia. Chinese traders traveled along this route, bringing their brightly colored silks to sell to merchants in the ports and cities of Europe.

contact with the West and with an empire as large as China's – Rome. From Chang-an, traders followed the Silk Road, crossing the smaller empires of Kushan and Parthia to reach the Mediterranean shores and the Roman world. Chinese silk fetched a high price, for the secret of making silk was unknown in the West.

Attacks from the Huns

Fearing attack from the Hsiung Nu or Huns, fierce horsemen from the north, the Chinese at first tried to buy them off with bribes. Under the strong Han emperor, Wu-ti (149–87 BC), the Huns came back to attack the Chinese capital of Chang-an, and there was savage fighting.

Wu-ti sent his armies west into central Asia to punish the Huns. While there, the Chinese reinforced their defenses. They rounded up large, fast horses for their cavalry. They added new stretches to the Great Wall to keep out the Huns. But over the years the Huns' repeated attacks weakened China. In AD 23, the nomads poured into China again and burned Chang-an. Han emperors reigned until AD 220, but their power was weakened. After Han rule ended, China, without a unifying ruler, split into several smaller kingdoms.

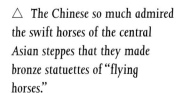

Green is the grass on the riverbanks/ Dense are the willows in the garden/ Fair is the woman upstairs/ Bright as the moon at her window.

ANONYMOUS HAN DYNASTY POEM c. AD 100

△ The Chinese so much admired the swift horses of the central Asian steppes that they made bronze statuettes of "flying horses."

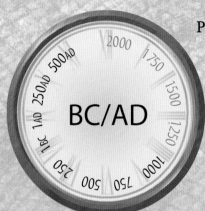

People from mainland Asia had settled on the islands of Japan by 7000 BC. The original inhabitants may have been the Ainu, about 15,000 of whom still live in Japan.

Japan

Rice farming begins in Japan.	1000 BC
Traditional date of Japan's first emperor, Jimmu Tenno.	660 BC
Start of the Yayoi period. Bronze and iron tools.	250 BC
Chinese visit Japan and report on its way of life.	AD 240
Growth of Yamato power in Japan.	AD 300
Japan probably unified under one ruler around this time.	AD 350
New ideas are brought from China. Japan rules part of Korea.	AD 400s
Yamato power declines. Japan loses its grip on Korea.	AD 500s

The early Japanese lived by hunting and fishing. Farming began around 1000 to 500 BC, when the Japanese learned to grow rice, a skill learned from China. They also began to make metal tools and to make pottery using a potter's wheel. The site in Tokyo where pottery from this time was first found gives this period of Japanese history its name: Yayoi.

Village life

The Yayoi farmers dug ditches to irrigate their rice fields. They built thatched homes and storehouses on stilts for their rice crop. Farmers lived together in villages, and each village was led by a chief who was often a woman shaman, or magician. The women shamans of Japan were powerful figures. In the 200s BC a shaman named Himiko used her authority to end a civil war between numerous small states. According to legend, Japan had its first emperor in the 600s BC but there is no historical evidence of his existence.

Contact with China

About AD 240, the Chinese sent ambassadors to the islands of Japan. These visitors wrote reports on what they saw,

▷ *A typical Yayoi farming scene, showing their thatched homes, storehouses on stilts and the ditches to irrigate their rice fields.*

BC/AD

2000 / 1750 / 1500 / 1250 / 1000 / 750 / 500 / 250 / 1BC / 1AD / 250AD / 500AD

▷ *The Chinese sent ships to report on what was going on in Japan. They called Japan "Wo," and regarded it as a subject country. Relations between the two countries seem to have been friendly, since Japan posed no threat to China.*

△ *A modern Ainu elder in traditional dress. A few Ainu people still live in separate village communities, following their traditional way of life, but most have integrated into modern Japanese society.*

giving historians the first detailed view of life in Japan at this time. The Chinese saw large towns and cemeteries - the Japanese buried their dead in large pottery jars or in stone coffins. The Japanese admired the Chinese and copied the way the Chinese wrote, the Chinese calendar, and the teachings of the scholar Confucius.

Warlords and emperors

By the AD 300s the Japanese had become expert in making iron tools and weapons. Shaman chiefs still ruled the villages, but there were now powerful warlords who led bands of warriors. These warrior-bands or clans (related families) fought for power.

Warlords were buried in huge tombs, beneath earth mounds, some of which were shaped like keyholes. The body of the dead ruler was laid to rest dressed in armor, with his weapons beside him, and with rich gold and jade jewelery.

By AD 400 one clan, the Yamato, had become supreme. They controlled central Japan and parts of southern Korea. The Yamato chiefs were the first real emperors and are regarded as the ancestors of Japan's present royal family.

Burying the dead

During Japan's Yayoi period, from 250 BC the dead were often buried inside wooden coffins or stone tombs. Stones were used to mark out the area of a burial site. Sometimes burial rites involved placing the body inside a double jar made of pottery, such as the one shown here. The tallest of these Japanese burial jars was more than 6.5 feet high.

△ *The Yayoi people made bell-shaped objects called dotaku out of bronze. They were decorated with pictures of animals or scenes from daily life.*

BC

The Celts came from central Europe, although their previous origins are unclear. Around 500 BC, perhaps to escape wars with their Germanic neighbors, they began to move westward. Groups of people settled in what are now Spain, France, Britain, and Ireland.

Celtic Europe

Some Celts, known to the Romans as Gauls, invaded Italy and others went as far east as Greece and Asia Minor. The Celts were warlike and their arrival usually led to fighting. In the British Isles, Celtic invaders sometimes drove out the local Britons, but elsewhere settled peacefully alongside them. They brought with them their languages, which became the Welsh and Gaelic still spoken more than 2,000 years later.

Warriors in hillforts

Celtic warriors fought in horse-drawn chariots and on foot, often with wild bravery. They were quarrelsome and often fought among themselves. But they were also skilled in farming and using iron to make tools and weapons.

To protect themselves and their farm animals, the Celts built forts on hilltops. Large family groups lived in or around these hillforts, taking shelter inside if attacked. The hillforts were oval or round, with earth ramparts topped by wooden stockades. The biggest, such as Maiden Castle in Dorset, had two or more ramparts and gateways defended by walls that curved out like horns, giving defenders a clear shot at anyone trying to break down the gate.

Evidence of Celts in Austria, from graves.	700 BC
Celts spread westwards across Europe, and also to the south and east.	500 BC
Celts attack and loot Rome.	390 BC
Romans counterattack and invade Cisalpine Gaul in northern Italy.	192 BC
Gauls and Romans fight for control of Massilia (Marseilles) in France.	100s BC
The Belgae, a Celtic tribe, move across the English Channel to settle in Britain.	75 BC
Julius Caesar tries to invade Celtic Britain, but withdraws.	55 BC
Caesar invades Britiain again. Celts agree to pay tribute (tax) to Rome.	54 BC

△ *A Celtic hillfort was surrounded by a ditch and an earth rampart topped by a wooden stockade. The round houses inside had conical thatched roofs and walls made of woven sticks plastered over with mud. The settlement's gateway was well defended against attack.*

△ *Around the campfire at night, Celtic poets, storytellers, and musicians would pass on tales of the gods and of events in the history of the Celtic people.*

Druids

Celtic priests called druids performed mysterious rites in sacred groves of trees. The Moon, the oak tree, and mistletoe were all magical to the Celts, and so too were many animals.

Art and legend

The Celts were artistic people. They loved stories and music, and they made beautiful jewelery and metalwork decorated with abstract designs and animal shapes.

They had no written language, passing on their legends of gods and heroes in stories around the fire. Most of what we know of the Celts comes from the writings of their enemies, such as the Romans. The Celts themselves left a legacy of art and legend, and language – Welsh, Breton, Cornish, Irish, and Scottish Gaelic are all Celtic languages.

Loyalty and sacrifice

The Celts were led by chiefs. Each warrior swore loyalty to his chief, who rewarded his followers with feasting and booty after victory. The various tribes never came together in a lasting state.

The Celts believed in many gods, some of whom were rather unattractive, such as pot-bellied Dagda, whose club could deliver either life or death. Celtic religion involved human sacrifice, although most reports of bloodthirsty practices come from the Romans, who thought the Celts were brave but barbarous.

Tempest on the plain of Lir/ Bursts its barriers far and near/ And upon the rising tide/ Wind and noisy winter ride –/ Winter throws a shining spear.

STORM AT SEA, CELTIC POEM

△ *The Celts were expert metalworkers, making fine objects out of gold, silver, and bronze. Their work featured geometric designs, animals, and human faces.*

BC

Rome grew from a small kingdom in Italy. It became a republic and one of the mightiest empires of the ancient world, with an empire stretching the length of the Mediterranean Sea.

The Rise of Rome

According to tradition, the city of Rome was founded in 753 BC. Legends say that early Rome was ruled by Etruscan kings, of whom Romulus was the first. Romulus and his twin brother Remus were suckled by a she-wolf after being abandoned by their wicked great-uncle. They founded Rome, but the brothers quarreled and Remus was killed.

Traditional date for founding of Rome.	753 BC
Roman Republic founded after overthrow of King Tarquinius Superbus.	510 BC
Plebeians (workers) revolt against patricians (aristocrats).	494 BC
Work starts on the Appian Way.	312 BC
Rome defeats Gauls, Samnites, and Latins in Third Samnite War.	298 BC
Patricians and plebeians share equal rights in Rome.	287 BC
Start of Punic Wars between Rome and Carthage.	264 BC
Carthaginian general Hannibal crosses Alps to attack Italy.	218 BC

The Etruscans, who came from Etruria in northern Italy, chose a strong position for their city on the top of seven hills. To the south lived the Latini, or Latins. In time both peoples became simply Romans.

The republic
In about 510 BC, the Etruscan kings were driven out of Rome, which became a republic. The Roman Republic was ruled by the Senate, which consisted of a group of elders who elected two consuls each year to lead them. The senators advised the consuls, but the consuls were powerful in their own right.

The typical Roman citizen was a peasant with a small farm. About 200 BC large estates owned by townspeople began to grow up, using slave labor.

△ A busy street in ancient Rome. Some buildings had several stories, and citizens collected water from a communal trough. Roman shops opened onto the street. Wine and oil sellers, butchers, and bakers did good business, and at times laws were passed to stop traders cluttering up the sidewalk.

△ Etruscan warriors. The Etruscans, the masters of central Italy in the 500s BC, were defeated by the Romans.

Roman Villa

A Roman villa was a large comfortable, country home, with hot-air central heating and a courtyard for fine weather. The family had servants to run the house and slaves to work on the farm.

The power of the army

Rome rose to power thanks to its fertile farmland, its army, and its key position in the middle of Italy. One of its earliest roads, the Appian Way, was built in 312 BC so that soldiers could travel southward. The Roman army was the best in Europe. By 200 BC Rome was Italy's leading power. It was able to challenge and defeat rivals such as Carthage for control of the Mediterranean world.

Everyday life in town and country

The Romans believed town and countryside should be organized and peaceful. They built walls around their towns for protection. Within the walls were shops and houses, both large and small. There were blocks of flats too. Rich and poor went to the public baths to wash, relax, and meet friends. Every town had its temples dedicated to protector gods and goddesses. Business was done in the forum, originally the town marketplace.

In the countryside, Romans lived with their servants in villas on big estates. Some villas were run as large farms. The owners kept sheep and cows, and vineyards were also profitable. The owner and his family lived in a comfortable house with its own garden.

He succeeded in founding his city, and installing the gods of his race in the Latin land... that was the origin of the Latin nation and the proud battlements of Rome.

THE AENEID, VIRGIL (70-19 BC)

Virgil was a Roman poet. He wrote his poem The Aeneid *to tell the mythical history of the founding of Rome by the poem's hero, Aeneas.*

△ Part of a carved stone relief depicting a Roman funeral procession. The pallbearers carry the dead person on a raised bier, followed by the mourners.

BC/AD

Having destroyed the power of Carthage in 201 BC, the Romans began to build an empire. The Celts, the Seleucid kings, the Greeks, and the Egyptians all fell before Roman power. Only the Parthians in the east and the Germanic tribes in northwest Europe defied the mighty Roman army.

The Roman Empire

After conquering Gaul, Julius Caesar invades Britain.	55 BC
Caesar is murdered.	44 BC
Romans conquer Egypt. Cleopatra and Mark Antony are defeated.	31 BC
Octavius becomes emperor and calls himself Augustus.	27 BC
Romans invade Britain.	AD 43
Volcanic eruption buries town of Pompeii in Italy.	AD 79
Roman Empire at its greatest.	AD 100
Barbarian attacks on Roman Empire increase.	AD 180
Visigoths attack Rome.	AD 410

Rome was a republic, with a form of democracy, but strong leaders were ambitious for sole power. In 49 BC Julius Caesar (100–44 BC) attacked Gaul. Like all successful Roman leaders, he knew that victory would bring booty, captives, and cheers from the people in Rome.

In 44 BC Caesar was murdered by plotters who feared he might become king. Civil war broke out. After the war Caesar's great-nephew Octavius, thereafter known as Augustus, became Rome's first emperor.

The empire

At its peak, the Roman Empire stretched from Britain in the west to Mesopotamia in the east. The army defended this empire. As well as fighting, Roman soldiers built roads, forts, and aqueducts. They guarded the borders while Roman ships patrolled the Mediterranean trade routes. A network of roads criss-crossed the empire, linking towns and forts.

Roman peace

Most people accepted Roman rule for the benefits it brought, letting them farm and trade in peace.

▷ Gladiators were trained to fight in the arena. Some carried a shield and sword; others fought with a net and a long three-pronged spear, or trident.

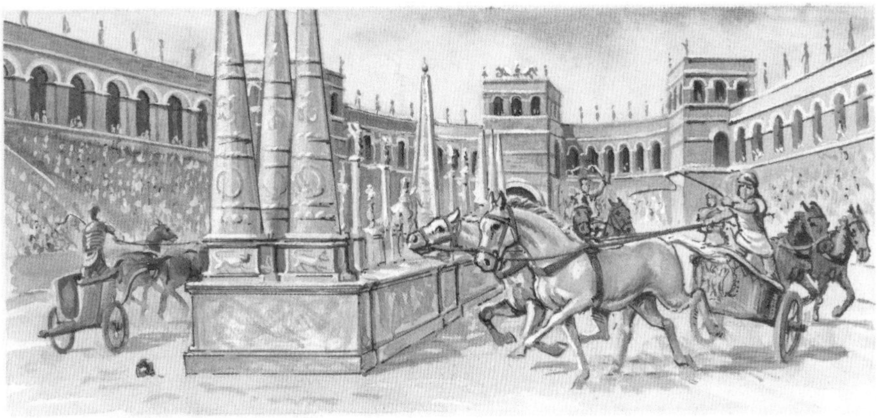

▷ The Circus Maximus in Rome was packed with fans of chariot racing. Races were fast and furious, with frequent violent crashes, and winning drivers became rich superstars.

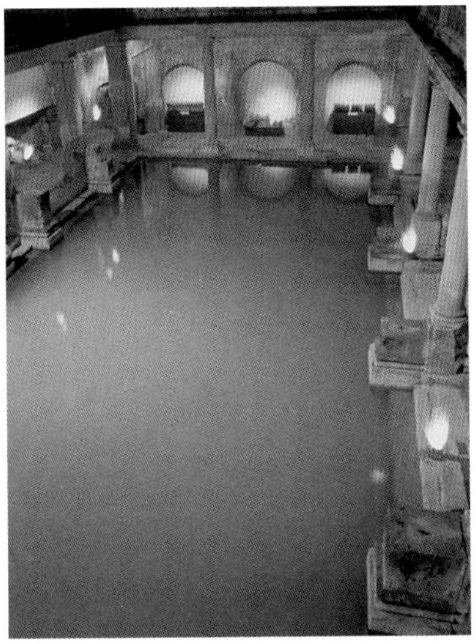

△ Part of the complex of Roman baths in the city of Bath, in England. Romans would visit the public baths to bathe in hot and cold pools, and also to relax and talk with their friends.

Towns grew, even in remote corners of the empire such as Britain. Wherever they went, the Romans built towns with baths, temples and theaters, and in the countryside, comfortable farmhouses called villas, many of which even had central heating.

To keep the mass of the people amused, Roman rulers presided over religious holidays, victory parades, and games in the arenas where mock battles and fights between gladiators were staged before vast, noisy crowds. Chariot racing was also popular, with heavy betting on races.

The Roman way

People throughout the Empire adopted Roman ways. Latin was widely used as the language of government, along with Greek, the language of scholars. Many people took to wearing Roman clothes and thought of themselves as Romans.

The Romans were great borrowers – they adopted many gods from other cultures, and they copied Greek styles in architecture and art. But they were also inventors. The Romans were the first to make concrete, and they used the arch to make roofs that spanned large inside spaces, without the need for columns.

A vast empire

Rome benefited greatly from its position in the middle of Italy. Through their economic power and by winning wars against their neighbors, the Romans were able to create one of the largest empires in history.

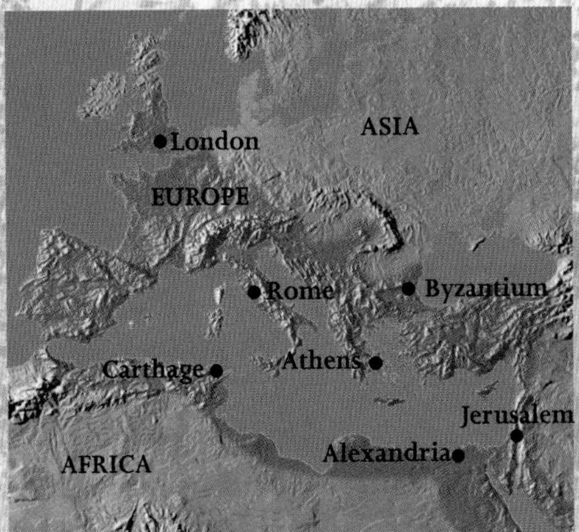
London
ASIA
EUROPE
Rome
Byzantium
Carthage
Athens
Jerusalem
Alexandria
AFRICA

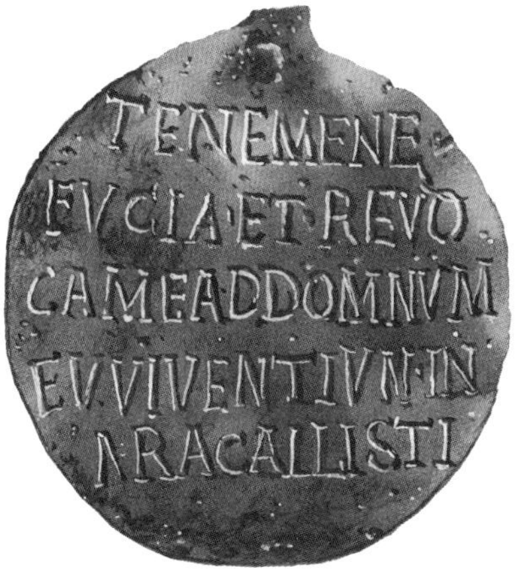
TENEMENE
FVGIA ET REVO
CAMEADDOMNVM
EVVIVENTIVM IN
ARACALLISTI

△ Slaves made up about a third of Rome's population. At the slave auctions, slaves wore tags advertising their skills and good character.

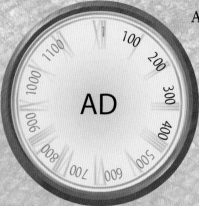

AD

At this time the Roman Empire was governed by the personal will of the emperor, but the emperor's power rested on the army. Weak or bad emperors were sometimes overthrown by army generals. Some emperors ruled well – Hadrian, for example, traveled widely to inspect building projects. Others, such as Nero and Caligula, were cruel or mad.

War and Government

Caligula is emperor.	AD 37–51
Claudius is emperor.	AD 41–54
Romans invade Britain.	AD 43
Colchester becomes a "colony" for retired Roman soldiers.	AD 49
Nero is emperor. Rome burns.	AD 54–68
Birth of Tacitus, a Roman historian who wrote about the conquest of Britain.	AD 56
Boudicca leads a revolt against the Romans in Britain.	AD 60
Vespasian, a former soldier in Britain, is emperor.	AD 68–79
Trajan is emperor. There are 31 legions, the highest number yet.	AD 98–117
Hadrian is emperor.	AD 117–138
The empire is divided.	AD 395
Rome is captured and burned by the Visigoths.	

The Romans were such good organizers that the empire usually kept working even when there was a fool at its center. It was divided into provinces, such as Britannia (Britain), each ruled by a governor or legate (chosen person). The governor had a staff of officials, who looked after finance, army matters, law-making, trade and all the other affairs of government.

The legions

The Roman army's main fighting troops were its legions. Each legion had up to 5,000 men, whose training and discipline were usually a match for any enemies they faced.

A legionary soldier wore armor to protect his body. On the road he marched at a steady pace, carrying his kit hung on a pole over one shoulder. He carried clothes, a food dish, cooking pot, rations, and tools.

▷ Most Roman soldiers fought on foot, although cavalry were used for patrols and in battle. Cavalrymen were sometimes recruited from foreign countries.

▷ Emperor Trajan (ruled AD 91–117) built a monument 100 feet high to the Roman army. Its carved reliefs show soldiers doing all kinds of tasks, from storming a fort to building a camp. This section shows Roman legionaries, who were builders as well as fighters, constructing a fort.

△ Octavian, a great-nephew of Julius Caesar, took the title Augustus as first emperor (27 BC to AD 14). The month of August was named in his honor.

Taking control

As soon as a new province was conquered, the army set up bases to control it. In Britain, the Romans invaded in AD 43, and having defeated the southern tribes, began building forts and roads.

When the eastern Britons rose in revolt under Queen Boudicca, the Romans were at first defeated, then regrouped and won a decisive victory. The Romans took revenge, burning farms and villages, but soon saw this was a mistake. They changed to "Romanizing" – making conquered Britain prosperous so that its people would no longer want to fight Rome. By AD 100, the Romans controlled England and Wales as far north as Hadrian's Wall in northern England.

Rome's power weakens

In the end, not even the Roman army could control such a huge empire. From AD 200 the army was stretched to defend the frontiers, especially in the east (Balkans) and northwest (Germany). Barbarian attacks increased. Britain was abandoned in the early 400s, soon after the empire had split into eastern and western halves. The western half crumbled, leaving the Eastern Empire, at Constantinople (now Istanbul Turkey), to preserve the legacy of Rome into a new age.

Hadrian's Wall

Hadrian's Wall was built in AD 122 to defend the northern frontier of Roman Britain. It acted as a checkpoint on movement between England and Scotland. The wall took eight years to build and stretches for 73 miles.

△ A Roman coin stamped with the head of the Emperor Hadrian. During his reign, he personally visited nearly every province in the Roman Empire.

BC/AD

The Greeks believed in many different gods, chief among these were a family of supernatural beings who lived on Mount Olympus and watched over humanity. Certain gods looked after the harvest; others cared for wild animals, the sea, war, and so on. The Romans took over many of these Greek gods and gave them Latin names.

Ancient Gods

The Greeks believed the gods could and did interfere in human affairs, bringing success or disaster. The king of the gods was Zeus, whom the Romans called Jupiter. The Greeks also believed that the Universe was a sphere. The upper half was light and airy, the lower half dark and gloomy. The Earth was a flat disc, floating between the two halves. When people died they went to the Underworld, which was ruled by Hades, the brother of Zeus.

Monsters and heroes

The Greeks also told stories about all kinds of nature spirits – magical beings often half-animal and half-human, such as centaurs (half-human

Mars   Minerva

and half-horse). There were fearful monsters that turned people to stone (such as Medusa), but even these horrors could be defeated by heroes, with the help of a friendly god or goddess. Some heroes in Greek myths, such as Odysseus and Jason, even became part of Western culture.

◁ *The Romans adopted Greek gods including Minerva (Athena, Greek goddess of wisdom and war). The Roman god Mars was identifed with Ares, the Greek god of war.*

First Olympic Games honor Zeus.	776 BC
Temples on the Acropolis in Athens are built.	400s BC
Socrates is sentenced to death for showing disrespect to the gods.	399 BC
Greece conquered by Rome. Romans adopt many Greek gods and myths.	146 BC
Probable year of Jesus's death. Christianity spreads into the Roman world.	AD 28
Many Romans switch from the old religion to new beliefs.	AD 100s
Persecution of Christians in Rome, during the reign of Diocletian.	AD 200s
Constantine makes Christianity the official religion of the empire.	AD 312

▷ A funeral procession passes along a Roman street. The body was carried on a litter for burial, followed by mourners and musicians. Noble Romans in particular honored their dead ancestors.

△ Ruins of Greek and Roman temples can be seen across Europe, the Near East, and North Africa. Every town had its own temple, dedicated to a protector god or goddess.

Gods and god-emperors

The gods of the Greeks and Romans were unpredictable and too much like humans in many ways. People tried to please the gods by building statues and temples in their honor and by offering gifts. Each city had its own protector god or gods. Athens was watched over by the goddess Athena. In Rome a huge temple to Jupiter stood on the Capitoline Hill. The gods were honored by processions and sacrifices carried out by a priest.

The Romans borrowed gods from all parts of their empire – from Greece, Egypt, Asia Minor, even Celtic Britain. Many soldiers became followers of Mithras, a Persian god. Several emperors were worshipped as gods while still living.

New and old ideas

Most Romans had no clear idea about what happened to people after death, although they were afraid of ghosts, and had a deep respect for ancestors. They were generally tolerant of new beliefs, but the Roman emperors did for a time persecute the new religion of Christianity. By the AD 300s many Romans had adopted the new faith, with its promise of an afterlife in heaven.

Sea god

Poseidon was the Greek god of the sea and is often shown carrying a three-pronged spear, called a trident. The Greeks believed Poseidon to be the brother of Zeus, the king of the gods, and Hades, god of the underworld. He was also associated with horses, and the Greeks thought that he was the father of the winged horse, Pegasus.

△ Zeus, king of the Greek gods. The first Olympic Games, which took place in 776 BC, were held in his honor. Zeus was head of a family of gods and goddesses called the Olympians.

The period from AD 500 to AD 1500 in Europe is known as the Middle Ages. It is called "middle" because it falls between the two worlds of ancient history and modern history, yet the term "Middle Ages" has no historical meaning in other parts of the world.

The Early Middle Ages

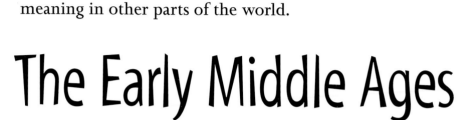

In China, for instance, history is described in terms of dynasties (ruling families), while the history of America is often divided into before Columbus (that is, before the arrival of European settlers) and after.

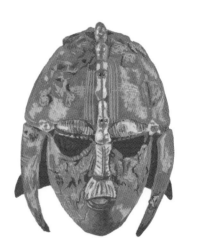

The world after Rome

Roman rule had created a common cultural framework across much of Europe, North Africa, and the Middle East. After the collapse of the Roman Empire, Roman ways continued to influence many people; Roman law, for example, became the basis for much European law. Latin, the language of the Romans, was used by scholars and in government. The Roman Catholic Church used Latin in its services until modern times.

So Roman culture lived on. Historians used to refer to the period after the fall of the Roman Empire as the "Dark Ages." Fine cities did fall into ruins, the old Roman roads crumbled, the Roman peace no longer existed. This was a time of movement, uncertainty, and violence. Yet it was not

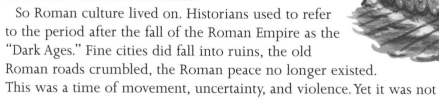

all darkness. Great works of art were created, achievements were made in science and architecture, and people performed great feats of heroism and exploration.

The new Europe

Although the Roman Empire in the West had fallen, the Empire in the East held out for a few hundred years. In Europe, the Christian Church was the force that held Europe together. The popes ruled from Rome, like the emperors of old. Christianity spread slowly across Europe, and in monasteries scholar monks preserved many Greek and Roman books for future generations.

A time of change

The early Middle Ages were a time of change. In the Middle East, the new and fast-growing faith of Islam became the backbone of new empires. In Asia, the empires of India and China continued to enjoy a civilization that was more advanced than any in Europe. People were on the move. Arabs and Turks expanded into new lands, Saxons and Angles moved across the North Sea to England. From Scandinavia, the Vikings set out in their longships across the seas to trade, farm, and fight.

The period covered by this book ends with the first millennium – and the Norman conquest of England in 1066. This marked a turning-point in the history of Britain, signaling an end to the ancient world. It opened the door to the second half of the Middle Ages, beyond which lay the Renaissance, the Age of Discovery and the dawn of the modern world.

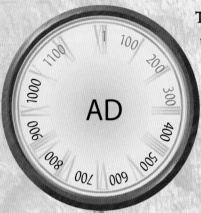

AD

The Roman Empire split in two in AD 395. After the collapse of the western half in AD 476, the eastern part survived. Its capital was Byzantium (now Istanbul in Turkey), a city founded by the Greeks.

The Byzantine Empire

The Roman emperor Constantine gave the city of Byzantium a new name, Constantinople. It became the home of eastern orthodox Christianity, and the capital of the Byzantine emperors.

Roman Empire divides into East (Byzantium) and West (Rome).	AD 395
Emperor Theodosius repairs and rebuilds the city walls.	AD 408
Fall of the Western Roman Empire.	AD 476
Justinian and Theodora rule Byzantine Empire.	AD 527–565
Byzantines conquer southeastern Spain.	AD 554
Wars with Arabs and religious quarrels weaken Byzantine power.	AD 700s
Byzantine Empire recovers.	AD 900s
Death of Basil II is followed by further period of weak rule.	AD 1025

Byzantium was "Rome in the East." Here, artists and scholars carried on the traditions of ancient Greek and Roman culture. The Byzantines loved music, poetry, and art, and decorated their churches with beautifully colored wall paintings, or frescoes, and mosaic pictures. Mosaics are pictures made from small pieces of glass or stone set in patterns.

Wars and laws

The Byzantine Empire was strongest in the AD 500s. The Emperor Justinian had a mighty general, Belisarius, who won many battles. He also had a clever wife, the empress Theodora. Justinian's laws, which gave new rights to women and children, became the framework for later legal systems in many countries in Europe.

A magnificent city

Most of the people of the Byzantine Empire were farmers. They came to the city to sell goods and to marvel. Foreigners visiting Constantinople were amazed by its magnificence. Its

△ Chariots raced around the track in the Hippodrome. Entrance was free (the emperors knew that the races kept the mob amused). *As well as thrilling and often dangerous races, there were animal fights, dancing girls, and circus acts to entertain the huge crowds.*

△ *A 19th-century print of the emperor Justinian and his influential wife Theodora. Through war and diplomacy, Justinian made Byzantium the greatest power in the eastern Mediterranean.*

Eastern empire

The Byzantine Empire swallowed up Turkey, the Balkans, parts of Spain and North Africa, Egypt, and the western coasts of the Mediterranean. The Empire was at its height under Justinian.

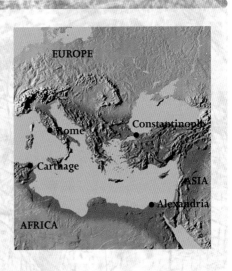

port was packed with ships, its markets swarmed with people of many nations. Richly dressed noblewomen were carried on litters by servants along streets in which slaves and soldiers jostled sailors and merchants.

The city was dominated by the enormous church of Hagia Sophia, to which the emperor and his retinue paraded to celebrate Christian festivals. Built in only six years, between AD 532 and 537, by order of Justinian, the huge domed building is one of the gems of world architecture. Inside the vast Hippodrome, crowds of 60,000 roared with approval or scorn for the chariot racers. Nobles and rich merchants lived in comfortable houses with central heating. Poor families crammed into multi-story tenement blocks.

As strong as its emperor

The Byzantine empire needed strong rulers. After Justinian's death in AD 565, few rulers came near to matching his power, and the empire was weakened by wars. Only vigorous soldiers were able to rally its forces and maintain a grip on its lands and trade.

Byzantium managed to fight off its enemies and survive into the second millennium. Its end came finally in 1453, when the city of Constantinople was captured by the Turks.

> Justice is the constant and perpetual wish to render to everyone his due.
> **EMPEROR JUSTINIAN (c. 482–565)**

△ *Byzantine traders used gold coins called bezants. These coins have been found across Asia as far as China and as far west as the British Isles.*

Most Native Americans were nomads, hunting for food. Yet in North and South America, and especially in Central America, people lived as farmers and built towns and cities.

Civilizations in the Americas

The most spectacular builders of North America were the Anasazi people, who lived in the southwest region of what is now the United States. They lived in cliffside "apartment blocks" called *pueblos*. Their descendants took the name of Pueblo. The Anasazi and their neighbors, the Hohokam, grew corn, wove cotton cloth, and made clay pottery.

Teotihuacan (Mexico) begins its rise to power.	AD 350
The city of Tiahuanaco (Bolivia) and Huari empire (Peru) are flourishing.	AD 600
In what is now the southwest U.S., the Anasazi build multi-story houses.	AD 700
The Mayan civilization is at its most powerful for the next 200 years.	AD 700
The city of Teotihuacan is destroyed. Tiahuanaco also declines about this time.	AD 750
Rise of the Toltecs in Mexico. They build a city called Tula.	AD 900
Chichén Itzá is the most important Mayan city and religious centre.	AD 900
The Mississippian people develop a farming culture in North America.	AD 1000

Teotihuacan

In Mexico, there stood one of the biggest cities in world. It was called Teotihuacan, or "City of the Gods," and it grew in the Teotihuacan valley from AD 350 to 750. The city had wide avenues, squares, palaces, and temples. These temples were built as step pyramids, and towered more than 195 feet high. The two largest are the Pyramid of the Sun and the Pyramid of the Moon. We know little about the city and what happened in it. It was conquered by the Toltecs who built their own temple-city at Tula.

Great mountain city

Over two miles high in the Andes Mountains, not far from Lake Titicaca, was the city of Tiahuanaco. It thrived between AD 500 and 1000. The kingdom of which it was part was ruled by priest-kings, who grew rich from farming and trade with nearby states such as Huari in Peru.

△ The Maya played a ball game in which players tried to knock a rubber ball through a stone ring. The game was both a sport and a religious rite, with the ball possibly representing the sun.

△ A temple in the Mayan city of Chichén Itzá. The city's natural well, called a cenote, was used for sacrifices. Many Mayan treasures have been recovered from the well, which was surrounded by pyramids, temples, and other buildings, including a ball court.

Priests and gods

A Mayan priest wears an elaborate feathered headdress. The Maya worshiped many gods. Priests led ceremonies in the pyramid-temples. Sacrificial offerings were made to please the gods, who included the jaguar.

The Maya

The Maya were at their most powerful from AD 200 to 900. Their calendars date back to before 3000 BC, and they remained powerful until conquered by the Spanish in the AD 1500s.

The Maya lived in city-states, ruled by kings who ruled over a society of priests, nobles, warriors, skilled craftworkers, and peasant farmers. Each city had its own sign, or emblem. Hunters in the forests brought birds' feathers, which were made into headdresses, and also jaguar skins, which were highly prized.

Mayan farmers grew beans, corn, and squash. They kept turkeys for meat and bees for honey, but they had no domestic animals that were big enough to pull wheeled carts.

Cities and sacrifices

The Maya built large cities. The biggest was Tikal (Guatemala), where about 60,000 people lived. Religious ceremonies and sacrifices (involving animals and sometimes humans) were at the center of Mayan life. Priests skilled in maths and astronomy studied the stars, the Sun and the Moon. The Maya used sign writing,

△ Chac, the Maya rain god. Carved stone figures called Chac Mools have been found in Mayan temples. They were probably used to make sacrificial offerings.

> Give us a steady light, a level place
> a good light, a good place,
> a good life and beginning.
>
> from THE POPUL VUH, ANONYMOUS MAYAN POEM

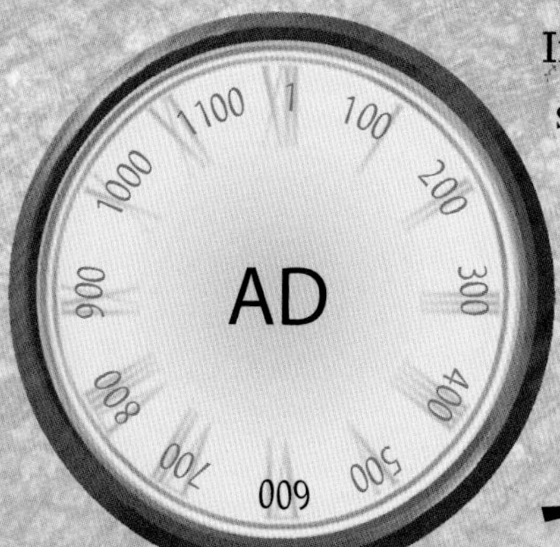
AD
1
100
200
300
400
500
600
700
800
900
1000
1100

In the first centuries after Christ, Christianity spread from Palestine into North Africa, Asia Minor, and across Europe. Further east, many people in the Arabian peninsula were still pagans, worshipping ancient gods. In this region, during the 600s, there arose a new religion – Islam.

The Rise of Islam

Probable date of Muhammad's birth.	AD 570
Muhammad begins preaching in Mecca.	AD 610
Flight to Medina, the Hegira.	AD 622
Muslims defeat the Meccans at Badr.	AD 624
Muhammad's teachings are written down in the Koran, the holy book of Islam.	AD 625
Meccans besiege Medina.	AD 627
Muhammad leads an army into Mecca and smashes the pagan idols there.	AD 630
Muhammad dies. Abu Bakr becomes the first caliph. Islam spreads beyond Arabia.	AD 632
Ummayad dynasty rules the Islamic world from Damascus.	AD 661

Islam had its roots in the Hebrew-Christian belief in one God, and its prophet was Muhammad (AD 570–632).

Muhammad's life and vision

Muhammad was born in Mecca (now in Saudi Arabia), an important trading town. After his parents died, he was raised by an uncle and became a merchant and caravan manager

Muhammad was angered by the evils he saw around him in Mecca: injustice, selfishness, and the worship of pagan idols. Many religious

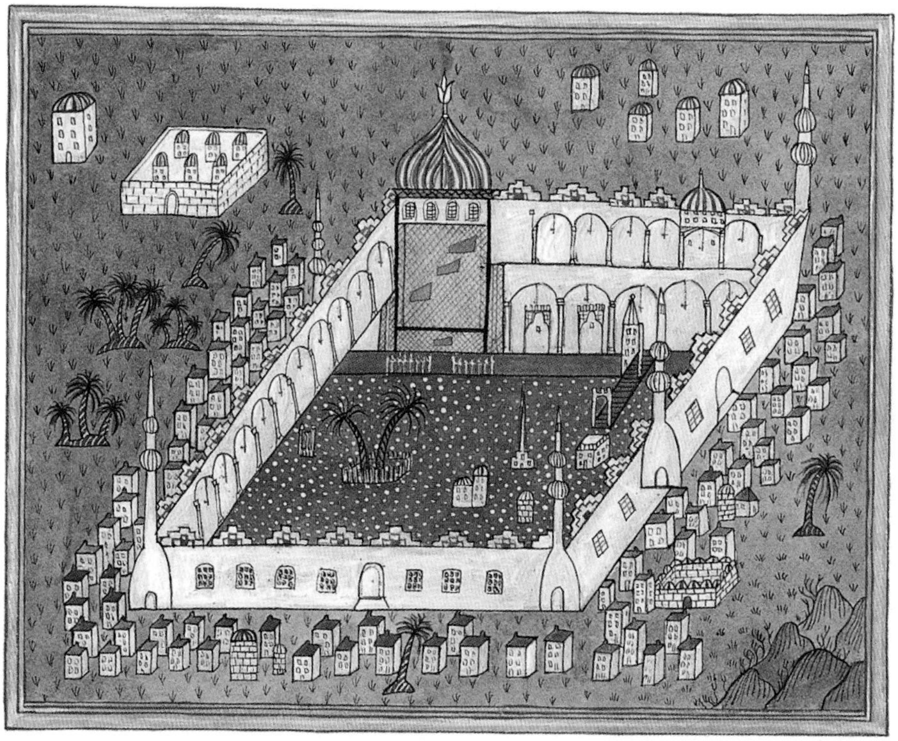

△ The old mosque at Mecca. Muhammad used to pray in the courtyard of his home. As a result, Islamic mosques have an open space where people gather five times a day to pray.

▷ The Muslims built mosques and minarets wherever the new religion took hold. One of the oldest Islamic monuments is the Dome of the Rock in Jerusalem (right), which was completed in AD 691. According to Muslim belief, Muhammad ascended to heaven from here to speak with God.

△ The people of Arabia traded by camel caravans, which broke their journeys at oases. Muhammad knew this life well. As a young man he worked as a manager for the caravans. He married his employer, a widow named Khadija.

ideas were talked over by travelers of many beliefs (including Jews and Christians) who met in the town to do business. Old beliefs were being questioned.

Muslims believe that the angel Gabriel came to Muhammad in a vision. The angel told Muhammad he must bring people to belief in the one true God, Allah, and to submission (Islam).

The birth of Islam

Muhammad began preaching and soon got into into trouble with the authorities in Mecca. In AD 622 he left the city, hid from his enemies in a cave, and then traveled across the desert to the town of Medina. This journey, known as the Hegira, begins the Muslim calendar. The Medinans welcomed him and adopted the new faith.

Many people in Mecca were determined to crush Islam. But in AD 630 Muhammad's forces entered the city in triumph. He broke up the pagan idols in the Kaaba, or shrine, but spared the Black Stone, which is still there. The Meccans submitted and Muhammad continued to preach and live frugally, until he died in AD 632.

Mecca became the holiest city of Islam. Muhammad's teachings were written down in the Koran, the holy book of Islam.

Astronomy

Astronomy was a respected science in the Islamic world, and Baghdad and other cities had flourishing scientific communities. Arab astronomers added their own observations to those of the Babylonians and Greeks and named many of the brightest stars.

△ Beautifully decorated tiles adorn the walls, domes, and minarets of mosques throughout the Islamic world. The brightly colored tiles feature geometric and arabesque patterns.

From the AD 500s, Japan was influenced more and more by Chinese ideas. The teachings of Confucius and Buddhism were brought to Japan. Prince Shotoku, who ruled from AD 593 to 622, strongly encouraged Chinese ways.

Fujiwara Japan

Shotoku believed that the Japanese emperor should be all-powerful, like the ruler of China. He made Buddhism the national religion, but the old Shinto religion continued to be strong, preserving a distinct Japanese identity.

Reign of Prince Shotoku, called the founder of Japanese civilization.	AD 593
Shotoku sends first Japanese embassy to China.	AD 608
Earliest written works in Japanese.	AD 700
Emperor Kammu makes Kyoto his capital.	AD 794
Bronze sculptures of Buddha made at the temple of Horyuji.	AD 800s
Fujiwara family gains control over the emperor.	AD 858
The Tale of Genji was probably written about this date.	AD 1008
Feuds weaken Fujiwara control. Power shifts to the daimyos.	AD 1000s

Prince Shotoku's changes

Shotoku reorganized the Japanese court into 12 ranks, and set out rules which governed the behavior of everyone from ruler to lowliest peasant. Shotoku's successors divided Japan into provinces, governed by local officials who reported directly to the emperor. In AD 794 emperor Kammu made Kyoto (then called Heian) his capital.

The Fujiwaras

In AD 858, however, the emperor lost control to a strong noble family called the Fujiwaras. The Fujiwaras had built up their power in the countryside, where they owned huge estates. Other nobles too had built up small 'empires' of their own.

The Fujiwaras gradually won control of the emperors, and of government, by marrying their daughters into the imperial family. The emperor had little real power. His Fujiwara "adviser" gave the orders.

△ At the court of the Fujiwaras, richly dressed men and women spent much of their time strolling in ornate gardens with flowering trees, artificial hills, and ponds.

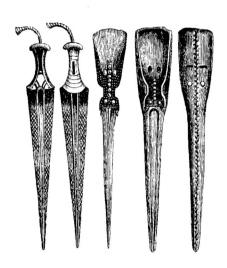

△ Japanese daggers. Iron weapons were made in Japan from the AD 300s, and were buried in nobles' tombs, with armor and models of servants and animals.

Samurai warriors

Japanese soldiers used iron swords and wore heavy armor. The bands of soldiers who served the land-owning loard, became known as the Samurai, the "knights" of medieval Japan.

The Fujiwaras held onto power in Japan for 300 years. During this time the great estates grew bigger and stronger, until the lords ruling them were almost like kings. By the AD 1000s, these lords, who were called daimyos, led private armies of heavily armored soldiers. These soldiers were called samurai.

Elegant court life

Fujiwara rule was based on life at court. Here, elegant courtiers wandered through beautiful gardens, or listened to poetry and stories. One of the most famous books in Japanese is *The Tale of Genji*, a long novel written by a court lady-in-waiting called Murasaki Shikibu in the early AD 1000s. Japanese writing was done with great care and skill, using a brush. The Japanese adopted Chinese writing to create their own written language, using characters to represent sounds. Only a few educated people could read Japanese.

Few ordinary people knew anything about this elegant life, unless they worked as servants at court. Most Japanese lived in small villages, as peasant farmers. They grew rice and vegetables, and caught fish from the sea. Small trading craft sailed between Japan and China, but otherwise Japan had little contact with the outside world.

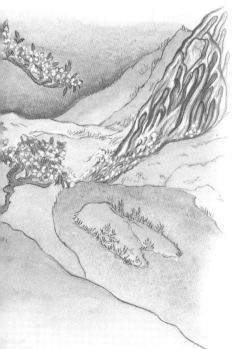

△ A wooden gate, or torii, is the symbol of Shinto, and stands outside Shinto temples. Shinto (meaning "the way of the gods") was the traditional religion of Japan.

Lady Koshosho, all noble and charming, she is like a weeping willow at budding time. Her style is very elegant and we all envy her manners.
DIARY OF MURASAKI SHIKIBU (c. AD 975–1031)

AD

After the end of Han rule in AD 220, China was weak and divided until AD 581 when Yang Chien founded the Sui dynasty (a series of rulers from the same family). He ruled from the city of Chang'an and governed well encouraging agriculture and foreign trade.

Chinese Dynasties

Chinese cities were a wonder to foreign visitors. Chang'an had more than one million citizens, yet its cleanliness was startling. There were public baths, and hot water was sold in the streets for washing. Toilet facilities in houses were fairly basic, emptying into cesspools, but waste was collected in carts every evening and taken away. The Chinese habit of using toilet paper came as another surprise to visitors.

The Tang and Sung dynasties

The second Sui emperor, Yang Di, was less prudent than Yang Chien. He taxed people heavily to pay for expensive projects, such as rebuilding the Grand Canal and constructing new imperial palaces and gardens. Discontent flared into revolt. The emperor was killed and a government official named Li Yuan seized power. He founded the Tang dynasty, which lasted for almost 300 years until it was overthrown by the warlord Chu Wen in AD 907.

End of Han dynasty is followed by a period of weak rule known as Six Dynasties.	AD 220
Start of Sui dynasty.	AD 581
The printing press may have been invented in China as early as this.	AD 600
Start of Tang dynasty. Period of prosperity and progress in arts and sciences.	AD 618
Northern rebellion is led by a soldier named An Lushan.	AD 755
More rebellions, leading to the fall of the Tang dynasty in 907.	AD 875–907
The Five Dynasties and Ten Kingdoms – leaders struggle for power in China.	AD 907–960
Sung dynasty founded. China's population tops 100 million.	AD 960

△ The wheelbarrow was a Chinese invention and was used by farmers, market traders, and construction workers. This typical barrow has a central wheel, not unlike today's garden barrows.

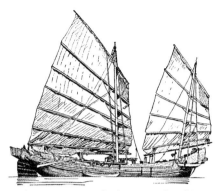

△ A two-masted Chinese junk. Chinese ships had watertight compartments and stern rudders. With easily handled sails, they were less sinkable and more easily steered than Western vessels.

△ The oldest printed book known is the Diamond Sutta, a Buddhist scroll made from sheets of paper printed with woodblocks. It was made in China in AD 868.

△ By AD 1100 the Chinese were using magnetic compasses such as this one, with an iron needle and marked points.

Making paper

A paper-maker at work, spreading wet pulp over a mesh frame. The invention of paper was announced by the director of the Chinese imperial workshops in AD 105. The Chinese began to use paper money under Sung rule.

For a time China was then split into five dynasties and smaller kingdoms, but in AD 960, the Sung dynasty reunited China and made their capital at Kaifeng. The Sung ruled until AD 1279. They were not as strong as the Tang emperors, but they were more technologically advanced.

Chinese culture

The Tang and Sung periods were good times for China. Painters and poets flourished. China was united and prosperous. Painters created beautiful calm landscapes, to show the harmony between people and nature. Poets such as Wang Wei, Li Po, and Tu Fu wrote about love and war. Potters made delicate pottery, known as porcelain. The Chinese were the first people to print books, using wood blocks.

Trade in China moved by road and along the impressive canals. The Grand Canal connected the main rivers. Most canals were dug in level ground, so avoiding the need for locks, but in the AD 900s Chinese engineers developed the pound-lock, with gates at either end, which could be emptied or flooded to let boats pass through.

New technology

The Chinese were fascinated by machines. They invented the wheelbarrow for carrying loads, and even fitted barrows with sails to make pushing easier. They used waterwheels to mill rice and drive hammers to beat metal into shape. They knew about the magnetic compass, and their ships had stern rudders (still unknown in the West). Chinese soldiers had the best crossbows in the world, and also a range of smoke and fire weapons. Most alarming of all to an enemy were rockets, which began to be used in the 900s, and "fireguns" – bamboo tubes filled with gunpowder.

Index